SCHIRMER'S LIBRARY
OF MUSICAL CLASSICS

WOLFGANG AMADEUS MOZART

Concertos

For the Piano

**Critically Revised, Fingered, and
the Orchestral Accompaniments
Arranged for a Second Piano**

K. 242 Lodron Concerto (J. Wagner)	Library Vol. 1578
K. 246 Concerto in C major (Philipp)	Library Vol. 1791
K. 271 Concerto in E♭ major (Philipp)	Library Vol. 1704
K. 413 Concerto in F major (Philipp)	Library Vol. 1788
K. 414 Concerto in A major (Philipp)	Library Vol. 1731
K. 415 Concerto in C major (Philipp)	Library Vol. 1789
K. 449 Concerto in E♭ major (Philipp)	Library Vol. 1756
K. 450 Concerto in B♭ major (Philipp)	Library Vol. 1746
K. 453 Concerto in G major (Philipp)	Library Vol. 1734
→ K. 456 Concerto in B♭ major (Philipp)	Library Vol. 1823
K. 459 Concerto in F major (Kullak-Philipp)	Library Vol. 1701
K. 466 Concerto in D minor (Kullak)	Library Vol. 661
K. 467 Concerto in C major (Bischoff)	Library Vol. 662
K. 482 Concerto in E♭ major (Bischoff)	Library Vol. 663
K. 488 Concerto in A major (York)	Library Vol. 1584
K. 491 Concerto in C minor (Bischoff)	Library Vol. 664
K. 503 Concerto in C major (Philipp)	Library Vol. 1786
K. 537 Concerto in D major (Rehberg)	Library Vol. 665
K. 595 Concerto in B♭ major (Philipp)	Library Vol. 1721

G. SCHIRMER, *Inc.*

DISTRIBUTED BY
HAL•LEONARD®
CORPORATION
7777 W. BLUEMOUND RD. P.O. BOX 13819 MILWAUKEE, WI 53213

Concerto in B♭ Major

for Piano and Orchestra

[K. 456]

Edited by
Isidor Philipp

Wolfgang Amadeus Mozart
(1756-1791)

II
f
II
II
fzp
p
II
fzp
p
fzp
p
II

II
p
f
p dolce

II
I
A
p
f

I
II

I
II
p

B
I
II
B
p
f
p
II
I
II
I
II

I
II
p
fp

I
II
fp
p

I
II
I
II
I
II

I
II
p
C
fz

I
II
tr
fz
p
fp

I
II
I
II
I
I
cresc.
tr
cresc.
f
f

II
f
II
II
p
II
f
I
p
II

D
p
I
II
D
p
p

I
II
tr
tr

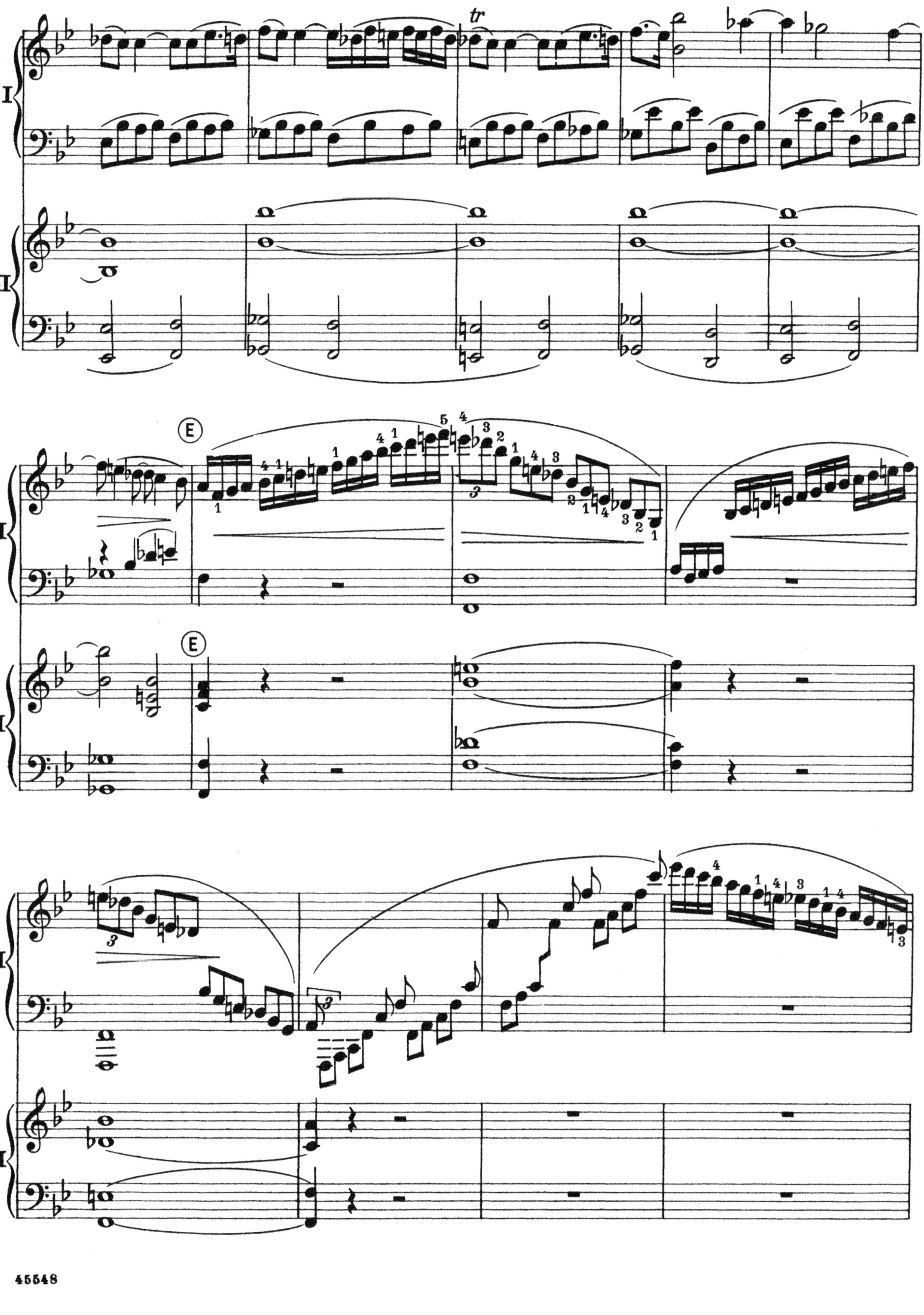
I
II
tr
E
E

I
II
p
cresc.
f
p
fp
tr
p

45548

F
I
II
f
p
p
F

I
II
fp
p

I
II
fp
fp
p

I
II
p

I
II
G
G
p
fz
fz

I
II
fz fz fz
p sf
I
II
fp
I
rf rf rf
fz
II
fp fp

H
I
II
p

I
II
tr
p cresc.
cresc.
f
tr

tr
II
II
I
p
II
I

I
I
I
I
f
l. h.
r h
l. h.
r. h.
l. h
r h
l. h.
I
sf
tr
tr

I
II
p dolce
II
II
II
f

Andante un poco sostenuto ♩ = 116
II
p
fz
fzp
fzp
tr
fz
tr
p
f
f
p

I
II
p
tr
5
3

I
II
fz
p

A
I
II
p
tr

II
fz
p
f
p
f
tr
p
B
I
II

I
II

II
fp
sf
C
I
p
tr
f

II
II
II
I
p
II

I
II
Maggiore
Maggiore
p

I
II
D
p

I
II
p
tr

E
I
II
p
tr
Minore
mf

I
II
mf

I
II
sf
p
cresc.
cresc.

I
II
p
fp
fp
fp
p
fp
fp
p
p
tr
F
F
p

I
II
pp
pp
I
II
I
II

Allegro vivace ♩. = 108
Allegro vivace ♩. = 108

II
II
II
II
II
f

II
p

A
tr
p
I
II
f

I
II
tr

I
II

I
II
p

B
B
I
II
I
II
I
II

tr
I
II

tr
C
I
II

45548

II
p
II
II
f
p
D
I
f
D
II

I
II

I
II
f
fp

I
II
f
p

E
tr
p
I
II

I
II
tr

I
II
I
II
I
II

I
II
F
F
p
p

I
II
tr
G
p

II
II
I
legato
II
I
I
11
11
11

I
II
I
II
I
II
cresc.
tr
f

I
10
14
I
I
I
I
tr

I
II
p
H

I
II
p
f

Alternate cadenza: First movement

p
p
sf
tr